THE REGISTRATION REVOLUTION

Are you Leaving money on the table?

The Entrepreneur's Guide to 12 Essential Indian Business Registrations that fuel Growth and Maximise Benefits

By

CA ASHUTOSH AGRAWAL

About The Author

CA Ashutosh Agrawal - Helping Business owners make the right decisions.

The Author, Ashutosh Agrawal, is not just a chartered accountant; he guides business owners on their growth journey.

With 7+ years of professional experience and exposure in saving losses for startups with zero turnovers to MNCs having thousands of turnovers, he is on a mission to provide immense value to businesses by helping them make the right decisions, growing exponentially, and helping in every next BIG STEP.

His passion for helping businesses grow stems from his zeal to add VALUE. While Business owners are excellent at developing and marketing their products, they often miss the regulatory actions that impact their business decisions, which often leads to losing more on interest and penalties than the revenue earned throughout business life. To save businesses from heavy setbacks and getting wound up, CA Ashutosh Agrawal has crafted 'The Registration Revolution' - A handbook for Businesses.

CA Ashutosh Agrawal is also a passionate teacher who has conducted many seminars and webinars for business owners, imparting key information at high times of need. His previous two webinars on 'Budget 2025' and 'Guide to Close books in March, Save Lakhs' were attended and praised by a good number of business owners.

CA Ashutosh Agrawal has been recognized by clients for the differences made in their growth journey. He is also recognized by the ICAI Raipur Branch for sharing his expertise in Advance Excel with CA Students in the early phase of their career.

More than a professional, CA Ashutosh Agrawal is a guide who helps businesses navigate through challenges in their growth journey, resulting in Immense Value addition to the business owner in making the right decisions.

About The Book

The Registration Revolution: The Entrepreneur's Guide to 12 Essential Indian Business Registrations.

Struggling to start your new Big business? Not sure about required registrations? You are not alone; currently, India is experiencing a growing trend with respect to startup culture. Every day, thousands of new ideas are born, but only a few hundred are executed. The reason is simple: They have no knowledge of how to start a business. The lack of curated information has killed more unicorns than built to date.

In the population of more than 140 crore Indians, there are very few professionals who guide the founder right. The business owner is a master in their field, but it's been seen that many lose big due to a lack of knowledge about the right steps.

This book will help YOU in -

- Taking informed decisions and making them right instead of trial and error.

- Analyzing yourself deeply and taking the right actions to correct mistakes made in the past.

- Adding immense value to your existing business, as even a single key point can save lakhs of rupees.

- Building brand, Growing Business, and Saving on Penalties - Ultimately increasing your Cash Inflow.

- Getting value-based services from the consultants.

This is a must-have handbook for every business owner because it promises to add value at every level of business. Every reader will surely get at least a key takeaway that will add immense value to their professional career. Use this handbook as your constant companion to guide you whenever you are stuck making any important growth decisions.

Are you ready for a new beginning on the Journey of growth by taking the first step and reading this book?

WHO IS THIS BOOK FOR? 

Is 'The Registration Revolution' the right book for you?

This 'Entrepreneur's Guide to 12 Essential Indian Business Registrations that Fuel Growth and Maximise Benefits' is NOT for everyone.

It's for those -

- Startup founders who want to make a unicorn and are not just testing the waters.

- Entrepreneurs who want to go global and are willing to take steps towards it.

- Business owners who want to launch an IPO are open to learning the right way of doing it.

- Salaried employees who want to make an impact on the job by helping employers execute growth-oriented work.

- Consultants who want to provide value-based service and not just compliance.

- Students of professional courses in the field of commerce who want to learn practical ways to practice the profession.

- Every person who always dreamed of owning a business but could not start due to lack of knowledge.

If you are one of these, then get ready to embark on the growth Journey. 'The Registration Revolution' is not just a book; it's a guide to getting your business where you aim it to be.

Acknowledgment

At the heart of this book lies a journey—one filled with experiences, learning, and the invaluable presence of people who have shaped my thoughts and supported me in ways I can never fully express. With utmost gratitude and humility, I take this opportunity to acknowledge the people and forces that made this book possible.

First and foremost, I bow with devotion to Lord Krishna. Whose divine guidance and inner presence have always been my strength in moments of confusion, doubt, and decision-making.

I am deeply grateful to my parents, whose values, sacrifices, and blessings have formed the foundation of everything I stand for. Their unspoken strength and quiet faith in me have been my deepest source of motivation.

To my wife, thank you for your boundless patience, constant support, and understanding throughout this Journey. Your encouragement gave me the strength to carry on, even when time and energy were stretched thin.

My siblings, with whom I have shared every phase of life—from childhood mischief to adult responsibilities—have been a source of love, honesty, and inspiration. Their presence in my life is a reminder of unconditional support that anchors me in every phase of growth.

I am fortunate to have found my coach and mentor, Mr. Gaurav Arora, whose clarity, guidance, and ability to challenge my thinking have helped me go beyond limits. This book is a result of his constant push, motivation, and guidance.

I am equally grateful to my clients, whose real-life challenges and scenarios pushed me to think deeper and provide practical solutions. In solving their problems, I have learned lessons no academic course could have taught me. Much of what is written here has emerged from those problem-solving experiences.

To my friends and professional colleagues, thank you for your encouragement, honest feedback, and thoughtful conversations that helped shape many parts of this book.

I also extend my appreciation to my office team, whose consistent efforts, discipline, and support in the background gave me the space and freedom to focus on writing with clarity and dedication.

And finally, to you—the reader—thank you. The idea of offering something meaningful to you has been the single greatest motivation behind this work. If this book contributes even a small insight, brings a little clarity, or solves one problem in your Journey, then every word written has been worth it.

With folded hands and a grateful heart,

— CA Ashutosh Agrawal

DISCLAIMER

This book is intended to provide general information and insights based on the Author's professional understanding and experience in the field of business, taxation, and regulatory compliance in India. It is meant for educational and informational purposes only and does not constitute legal, financial, or professional advice.

While every effort has been made to ensure the accuracy and reliability of the content as of the date of publication, laws and regulations are subject to change. Readers are strongly advised to consult with a qualified professional or legal advisor before making any decisions or taking action based on the information contained in this book.

The Author and publisher disclaim any liability, loss, or risk incurred—directly or indirectly—by the reader or any other person as a consequence of the use or application of any of the information presented herein.

Any references to specific government portals, departments, laws, schemes, or processes are for illustrative purposes only and may be subject to procedural or policy changes.

The views expressed in this book are solely those of the Author and do not reflect the views of any institution or organization the Author may be affiliated with.

All trademarks, product names, company names, and logos mentioned in this book are the property of their respective owners and are used for identification purposes only.

TABLE OF CONTENT

CHAPTER 1

START WITH THE BASICS

This might seem like a very common topic, but trust me when I tell you that even today, a large chunk of the country's earning population has not yet applied for a Permanent Account Number (PAN).

This Chapter is not just about applying for PAN, but we will also discuss key points to keep checking your PAN and the importance of keeping it updated.

Let's first start with understanding from the basics -

What is PAN?

PAN stands for Permanent Account Number. PAN is a ten-digit unique alphanumeric number issued by the Income Tax Department. Given below is an illustrative PAN: **ALWPS5809L**

Benefits of PAN

A PAN has been made compulsory for every transaction with the Income-tax Department. It is also mandatory for numerous other financial transactions such as the opening of bank accounts, deposit of cash in a bank account, opening of DEMAT account, transaction of immovable properties, dealing in securities, etc. A PAN card is a valuable means of photo identification that is accepted by all Government and Non-Government institutions in the country.

How to read a PAN

PAN is a ten-digit unique alphanumeric number issued by the Income Tax Department. The formation can be better understood with the Example of Mr. Akhil Sharma, whose PAN is **ALWPS5809L** :

Out of the first five characters, the first three characters represent the alphabetic series running from AAA to ZZZ. (E.g. **ALW**PS5809L).

The fourth character of PAN represents the status of the PAN holder (E.g. ALW**P**S5809L).

"A" stands for Association of Persons (AoP)

"B" stands for Body of Individuals (BOI)

"C" stands for Company

"F" stands for Firm/Limited Liability Partnership

"G" stands for Government Agency

"H" stands for Hindu Undivided Family (HUF)

"J" stands for Artificial Juridical Person

"L" stands for Local Authority

"P" stands for Individual

"T" stands for Trust

The fifth character of PAN represents the first character of the PAN holder's last name/surname in the case of an individual. (E.g., Mr. Akhil Sharma - ALWP**S**5809L).

In the case of non-individuals, For Example, a partnership firm - **G**upta and Associates PAN's fifth character will be the first character of the entity's name, i.e., ALWF**G**5809L

The next four characters are sequential numbers running from 0001 to 9999 (E.g. ALWPS**5809**L).

The last character, i.e., the tenth character, is an alphabetic check digit (E.g. ALWPS5809**L**).

The combination of all the above items gives the PAN its unique identity.

Mandatory Requirement of PAN

Below mentioned are cases when it is mandatory to have PAN -

a. Every person, if their total income exceeds the maximum amount, is not chargeable to tax (Currently, the limit is Rs 250,000).

b. A charitable trust.

c. Every Business owner whose turnover is likely to exceed five lakh rupees in the financial year.

d. Every non-individual entity (Firm, Company, etc.) if the financial transaction during a financial year exceeds Rs. 2,50,000.

e. Every person associated with the entity mentioned above is a managing director, director, partner, trustee, author, founder, karta, chief executive officer, principal officer, or office bearer.

f. Every person entering into any transaction is mentioned in the following points.

Transaction where quoting PAN is Mandatory

As per rule 114B of the Income Tax Act 1961, the following are the transactions in which quoting of PAN is mandatory by every person -

a. Sale or purchase of a motor vehicle.

b. Opening an account with a bank.

c. Making an application for a credit or debit card.

d. Opening of a DEMAT account.

e. Payment in cash of an amount exceeding Rs. 50,000 to a hotel or restaurant against a bill at any one time.

f. Payment in cash of an amount exceeding Rs. 50,000 in connection with travel to any foreign country or payment for purchase of any foreign currency at any one time.

g.   Payment of an amount exceeding Rs. 50,000 to a Mutual Fund for the purchase of its units or to a company or an institution for acquiring debentures or bonds.

h.   Cash Deposit with a bank exceeding Rs. 50,000 during any one-day

i.   Investment in Fixed Deposit exceeding Rs. 50,000 in one transaction or totaling more than Rs. 5 lakhs during a financial year.

j.   Payment of an amount aggregating to more than Rs. 50,000 in a financial year as a life insurance premium to an insurer

k.   Sale or purchase, by any person, of shares of a company not listed in a recognized stock exchange for an amount exceeding Rs. 1 lakh per transaction.

l.   Sale or purchase of any immovable property for an amount exceeding Rs. 10 lakh.

m.   Any other Sale or purchase of goods or services not specified above for an amount exceeding Rs. 2 lakh per transaction.

What if the default is made with provisions related to PAN?

Section 272B of the Income Tax Act 1961 provides for a penalty of Rs. 10,000 per case to be levied for default of not obtaining PAN, knowingly quoting incorrect PAN, intimating incorrect PAN to the person deducing tax or person collecting tax.

Can a person hold more than one PAN?

A person cannot hold more than one PAN. If a PAN is allotted to a person, then he cannot apply for obtaining another PAN. A penalty of Rs. 10,000/- is liable to be imposed under Section 272B of the Income-tax Act, 1961, for having more than one PAN.

If a person has been allotted more than one PAN, then he should immediately surrender the additional PAN card(s).

Having understood the important details about PAN, I'm sure now everyone will correct all the mistakes they have made unknowingly.

****

Let me share with you an interesting, practical

Case Study,

Mr. Alok, a disciplined salaried professional, had obtained his Permanent Account Number (PAN) early in his career and consistently filed his income tax returns in India. All his compliances were done on time, and his records remained clean.

After working for over a decade, he received a lucrative opportunity abroad and moved to the USA, where he eventually settled. Since he no longer had any taxable income in India, he naturally stopped filing Indian returns. However, he continued to maintain a few properties back home.

Years later, while in the middle of negotiating the sale of one of his Indian properties, Mr. Alok received a sudden email from the Income Tax Department of India demanding a tax payment of ₹80,000. The notice came as a shock. He had not earned any income in India for years — how could there be a demand?

Upon further investigation with his tax consultant, an alarming issue surfaced:

Mr. Alok's PAN had been erroneously linked to another individual with the same name — Alok (referred to here as Alok-2).

Alok-2, a salaried individual residing in India, had been issued the same PAN erroneously and was using it for filing returns regularly. In one of the assessment years, an error in filing had resulted in a tax demand of ₹80,000, which was now erroneously reflected against Mr. Alok (original).

Because of this unresolved demand, the property sale was stalled, and the buyer eventually withdrew. What followed was eight months of continuous correspondence and legal clarification before Mr. Alok could prove his true identity and clear the PAN linkage.

Key Takeaway

This case underscores the critical importance of maintaining oversight of one's PAN record, even when no longer residing in India.

A single error or overlap—even one not committed by you—can result in serious consequences, including litigation, blocked transactions, and financial loss.

A PAN is more than just a tax number — it's a lifelong financial identity that must be protected and periodically reviewed.

****

Many business owners get confused between PAN and TAN; we have discussed in detail the requirements, benefits, and uses of PAN. TAN is not required by every business person; whenever a business incurs liability to deduct TDS or collect TCS on their payments and receipts respectively, only then do they have to apply for TAN. In simple words, most businesses will be liable to get TAN if their annual turnover is more than Rs. 1,00,00,000 /-.

CHAPTER 2

FASTER MONEY, STRONGER BUSINESS

Manufacturers and Service Providers are facing big challenges in recovering the dues from Debtors. They also believe it's impossible to get a loan from a bank in the absence of collateral security.

What if I tell you that all this is not true. This Chapter will reduce your debtor credit period to 45 days only.

As per the MSME Act 2006, A business is classified under **Micro, Small, or Medium Enterprises** as per the following criteria (with effect from 01-04-2025) -

Classification	Based on Investment in Plant and Machinery	Based on Annual Turnover
Micro	Up to 2.50 Crores	Up to 10 Crores
Small	Up to 25 Crores	Up to 100 Crores
Medium	Up to 125 Crores	Up to 500 Crores

The government regularly makes policies to promote MSME enterprises because it understands that they are the backbone of the Indian economy. We can only achieve the Goal of a 5 Trillion dollar economy when the MSME sector is strong.

Today, a major challenge an MSME is facing is the availability of funds. There are enormous expansion opportunities, but due to the inability to obtain enough funds at the right time, businesses are unable to tap into those opportunities and eventually collapse.

****

Take the story of Ravi, who ran a small manufacturing unit in Indore. His products had started gaining popularity, and he received a large export order — a golden opportunity to scale his business and enter international markets.

However, Ravi faced a major roadblock: he needed additional working capital to procure raw materials and scale production.

Despite having confirmed orders, he struggled to get timely funding from banks, who were hesitant due to his limited financial history and lack of collateral.

By the time funding options materialized, the export order was withdrawn. The opportunity slipped through his fingers. Eventually, Ravi's Business couldn't sustain the pressure of missed opportunities and rising debts, leading to its closure.

****

To tackle these challenges, the Government has launched many **beneficial schemes** like -

1. Government Guarantee Credit Scheme

Under this scheme, loans of up to Rs. 10 Crores will be sanctioned to eligible MSME businesses without the mortgage of any collateral property. The Central Government gives guarantees against such borrowed funds. This benefit is available to all types of businesses - Manufacturing, Trading, or Service providers.

2. Mandatory dues recovery within 45 days

MSME Act 2006 has provided a big relief to Manufacturers, or Service Providers registered as Micro or Small enterprises; they need not worry about the recovery of dues against credit sales.

As per the Act, debtors have to pay interest at the rate of 3 times the RBI rate of interest (Currently, it comes to around 20% pa) in case of delay in payment beyond 15 days (without written agreement) or 45 days (with an agreement) to MSME registered businesses. There is no provision for waiver of this interest liability.

Additionally, As per Section 43B(h) of the Income Tax Act 1961, if the debtors make payment beyond the timelines discussed above, their expenses will be disallowed along with interest liability thereon.

3. Subsidy on Fees

MSME Registered entities have to pay subsidized fees for Trademark or Patent registration. A subsidy of 50% is available to MSME-registered entities.

4. MSME Samadhan

This portal was developed by the government to enforce the implementation of rules and ensure that MSME entities do not suffer. When an entity is eligible for the 45-day rule, and interest payment is not paid, they can file an application against a debtor in MSME Samadhan, wherein quick resolution is provided.

These benefits provide an initial boost to the business so that it can focus on growing rather than worrying about cash flows.

Registration under the MSME portal is a simple process, and no government fees are payable. Entities can register their Business under MSME at www.msme.gov.in.

Earlier classification criteria were low, but in the Finance Budget 2025, the Government has increased the limits. So, more and more businesses can benefit from this scheme.

CHAPTER 3

NEW FAMILY MEMBER

What if I tell you there is a legal way for you to have an additional family member for income tax purposes, and you can save additional tax on income up to Rs. 4,00,000 /- (From FY 2025-26)?

Yes, you read it right; there is a concept of Hindu Undivided Family (HUF) under the Income Tax Act 1961 in which Income up to Rs. 4,00,000 /- is tax-free under the new scheme. Let's now understand How?.

Income Tax recognizes the concept of HUF from Hindu law; this also extends to Jains, Buddhists, and Sikhs. As per Hindu law, HUF is created automatically after the marriage of two individuals, but the income tax act requires a minimum of two coparceners (members of HUF by birth) to recognize an HUF.

This implies that as per the Income Tax Act 1961, HUF comes into effect after the birth of the first child; before the year 2005, only the birth of the male child was recognized for this purpose.

After the amendment of Hindu Law in 2005, HUF was recognized after the birth of either a son or a daughter.

HUF is considered a separate legal entity. The income of HUF is computed on its PAN and taxable at slab rates, similar to individuals.

HUF is mostly used for succession and Tax planning.

HUF can, in its own name:

1. Operate a bank account.

2. Own a property.

3. Do a Business

4. Have a separate DEMAT account.

5. Earn business income, rental Income, capital gains, interest income, or any other source income.

****

We can understand the power of HUF better with the help of a case study -

Let's say Mr. Manav is a happily married individual. He is earning salary income and also runs an online business. He gets rental Income from a house property and also earns interest on investments.

He also makes some income from the sale of shares. So, for FY 2024-25, Mr. Manav's income is computed as follows, and tax liability is also ascertained.

Particulars	New Regime
Income From Salary / Business	1,875,000
Standard Deduction	75,000
Net Taxable Income from Salary	1,800,000
Rental Income (Income From House Property)	600,000
Less 30%	180,000
Net Rental Income	420,000
Income From Business and Profession	200,000
STCG From Share Market (Sold before 23-07-2024)	100,000
Interest from FDs, Bonds, Dividend, Savings Bank Interest	200,000
Total Income	2,720,000

Tax	5,10,640
Effective Tax Rate	18.77%

Now, let's consider a scenario where Mr. Manav earns only salary income in his PAN, and all other Income is earned in the PAN of HUF.

Particulars (Mr. Manav)	New Regime	Particulars (HUF)	New Regime
Income From Salary / Business	1,875,000	Rental Income (Income From House Property)	600,000
Standard Deduction	75,000	Less 30%	180,000
Net Taxable Income from Salary	1,800,000	**Net Rental Income**	420,000
Total Income	1,800,000	**Income From Business and Profession**	200,000

Tax	239,200	STCG From Share Market	100,000
Total Tax (Manav + Manav HUF) - Rs. 2,88,080/- [2,39,200 + 48,880] Effective Tax Rate - 10.60% Tax Saving - Rs. 2,22,560 /- [5,10,640 - 2,39,200]		Interest from FDs, Bonds, Dividend, Savings Bank Interest	200,000
		Total Income	920,000
		Tax	48,880

This is how useful an HUF can be. As we have seen in the case study above, Mr. Manav saved approximately Rs. 2.20 lakhs of tax by using the concept of HUF.

****

However, it is advisable to plan this under professional consultancy as any error in compliance can cost huge. A few key points with respect to earning Income HUF are -

1. As discussed earlier, a minimum of two coparceners are required to assess HUF's Income under the Income Tax Act 1961.

2. There is a concept of coparcener; coparceners are part of HUF by blood relation, and they have the right to demand their share of the property of HUF.

3. HUF consists of Coparceners and Non-Coparceners (Wife of karta of HUF) called Members of HUF. Members are considered relatives of HUF as per the Income Tax Act 1961. Any amount of gift from relatives is tax-free, but a clubbing provision applies wherein income earned by HUF from gifts received from relatives will be taxed in the hands of members who are gifted to HUF.

Considering the key points, it is again advised to seek professional assistance before undertaking the task of HUF formation.

****

Earlier in the Chapter, we also discussed how HUF can be used as a succession planning tool. We will understand this topic with an

Example.

Mr. and Mrs. Sharma, a financially prudent couple from Jaipur, built a comfortable life over the years. As part of their long-term investment strategy, they purchased a prime commercial shop in a bustling market area.

The shop was not only appreciated in value but also provided steady rental Income. Over time, they also acquired some other investments and movable assets.

They had three children, all well-settled and pursuing independent careers. During their lifetime, Mr. and Mrs. Sharma managed the shop jointly and treated it as part of their family estate.

However, no formal structure was put in place to govern the ownership or succession of the property.

After Their Demise: A Valuable Asset, a Family Divided

Following the demise of both parents, the three siblings found themselves in disagreement over the ownership and use of the shop:

- No one wanted to sell it — the location was too premium and emotionally significant.

- At the same time, none of them could individually claim it, nor did the others want to hand it over to one.

- Rental Income was stuck, and no one could lawfully collect or reinvest it without everyone's consent.

- What had once been a unifying family asset had now become a source of dispute and stagnation.

How HUF Could Have Helped

Had Mr. Sharma formed a Hindu Undivided Family (HUF) and brought the shop and assets under the HUF structure, the situation could have been managed very differently:

- Upon the demise of the parents, the HUF would have continued as a going concern.

- All three children would have automatically become coparceners, each having an equal right in the HUF property.

- Rental Income could have continued under a shared, legally structured framework.

- Disputes over ownership and Management could have been addressed through mutual decision within the HUF rather than litigation or stalemate.

****

Conclusion

This case reflects a common yet avoidable situation.

Without proper succession planning, even the most well-intentioned family assets can become a cause of division.

A Hindu Undivided Family is not merely a tax-saving tool — it can serve as a practical and culturally rooted succession vehicle, preserving family wealth and ensuring smooth intergenerational transfer.

CHAPTER 4

GOOD AND SIMPLE TAX

Even after 8 years of the launch of the **Goods and Service Tax Act**, businesses feel that it's a big challenge to ensure complete compliance with the Act. No matter how much work they do, they are bound to get the notices. Even many small businesses are still afraid to get registered under the Act.

After reading this Chapter, your beliefs will change, and you will start taking most benefits out of the GST Act without worrying about the compliance challenges.

When I tell this at a public gathering, many wonder what the benefit of GST is. If you are one of them, then you are in for surprises.

1. <u>Goods and services tax offers an 18% discount on Expenses.</u>

Let's understand this with a story -

Meera and Kavita were both passionate fashion designers. They started their own clothing boutiques in the same market, using similar suppliers and marketing channels.

Kavita chose to keep her business small and did not register under GST.

Meera, though not crossing the threshold, opted for GST registration voluntarily.

Both of them bought fabrics, designer materials, sewing machines, and packaging materials and paid for advertising and rent.

Let's say they each spent around ₹10 lakhs annually on such inputs, which attracted 18% GST.

Expenses Breakdown

Kavita (Unregistered):

She paid ₹10 lakhs + ₹1.8 lakhs GST = ₹11.8 lakhs.

She couldn't claim any ITC, so the ₹1.8 lakhs GST was an added cost.

Meera (Registered):

She paid the same ₹11.8 lakhs, but she claimed ₹1.8 lakhs as Input Tax Credit while filing her GST returns. This brought down her effective cost to just ₹10 lakhs.

The Result

Meera enjoyed an 18% advantage on every eligible business expense. She could either offer more competitive pricing or invest the savings in growing her business.

Kavita, on the other hand, had to either pass on the tax burden to her customers (making her products costlier) or absorb it and reduce her profit margins.

Conclusion

This story shows how the Input Tax Credit under GST effectively offers a built-in discount on business expenses, making GST registration not just a compliance requirement but a strategic financial benefit.

****

2. <u>Market Credibility</u>

Businesses have reported getting easy lead conversion because they were registered under GST.

This is because GST registration builds an automatic reputation for even new businesses in the market.

Any new business faces challenges in convincing prospective customers of its credibility; the reason is that customers are not sure about the business's capabilities in catering to their needs due to a lack of experience.

When a new business is registered under GST and maintains a strong compliance record, customers get assured about the genuineness of the business.

3. <u>Strong Compliance Rating</u>

Section 149 of the CGST Act covers the concept of Compliance rating. When a business files all the returns in a timely manner and dues are paid without delay, its compliance rating will be high.

As per the Act, these compliance ratings will be available publicly for any businesses. When a supplier files their GSTR 1 in a timely manner, only the recipient gets ITC.

The concept is that during any new deal, the recipient will check the supplier's compliance rating before finalizing the deal. A good compliance rating will help close deals quickly.

Currently, even though the Compliance rating tab is active under the Profile menu. It currently does not show any rating.

4. __Unrestricted entry into associations__

Business owners become part of their industries' trade associations to get many benefits out of it. A few of the many benefits that businesses get from associations are that they are able to get their concerns resolved, common issues are solved, and representations are made at various levels on behalf of the industry.

It has been seen that GST registration is mandatory for membership in many reputed trade associations.

Therefore, GST registration will also help businesses in becoming a part of the community.

5. __Easy sale to MNCs__

Nowadays, many multinational companies and corporations have a concept of vendor registration before buying material or services from any person. Under that vendor registration process, they have defined a mandatory policy that requires vendors to be registered under GST. Here, an unregistered supplier will also lose a business opportunity, and a registered vendor will easily qualify for the criteria and get the business.

These are a few major benefits that a business enjoys when registering under the GST Act.

The government has not made it mandatory for every business to register under the Act; the criteria is that in the case of a supplier of Goods, Registration is mandatory if turnover exceeds Rs. 40 lakhs, and for Service Providers, the limit is Rs. 20 lakhs.

There are cases separately mentioned under Section 24 of the CGST Act 2017 where turnover limits will not apply and registration is mandatory. Those cases are -

1. Inter-State supply.

2. Casual Taxable Person

3. The person having liability under the Reverse Charge Mechanism

4. E-Commerce Businesses

5. Non-Resident Person making taxable supply

6. GST TDS deductors

7. Agency Businesses

8. Input Service Distributors

9. Person supplying through E-Commerce operators

10. Every person supplying online information and database access or retrieval services from a place outside India to a person in India

11. Every person supplying online money gaming from a place outside India to a person in India

Having understood the rules where GST registration is mandatory, it is recommended that every business having B2B (Business to Business) supplies should get registered under GST to get most of the benefits discussed above.

CHAPTER 5

INCORPORATE LEGACY

Many MSME businesses believe that the Company is for big businesses, and it's a big compliance headache. What they miss is the immense benefits a company can bring to businesses.

Every business follows a cycle and goes through ups and downs. In bad times, a company will be the biggest savior of a business owner's personal wealth. In good times, it will also save from huge taxes by providing flat tax rates.

Let's delve into the details of how a **company** can work.

A company is a separate legal entity. Just as an individual has his identity proofs like an Aadhar Card, a company has its own identity, which is called a Certificate of Incorporation.

The Company operates under some policies defined in documents called Memorandum of Association (MOA) and Article of Association (AOA). MOA Defines 'What' a company will do, and 'AOA' Defines 'How a company will work.

The Company is owned by Shareholders and Managed by Directors. Directors are responsible for day-to-day decision-making for the

Company, and they report to the Shareholders either Quarterly or Annually, depending on the size of the Company.

Now, you may be wondering how a company will save the owner in Bad times?

A company is a Limited Liability entity, unlike a Proprietorship or Partnership, which has unlimited liability.

****

Let's understand this better with an Example,

Ramesh and Suresh were childhood friends who decided to start their own businesses.

Ramesh chose to run a proprietorship selling electronics.

Suresh decided to register a Private Limited Company offering similar products.

Both businesses did well initially. However, after a couple of years, both faced an unexpected challenge — a large consignment turned out defective, and both received heavy legal claims and losses amounting to ₹25 lakhs.

What happened next?

In Ramesh's case (Proprietorship):

His personal assets — house, savings, and car — were all at risk. Since a proprietorship does not distinguish between personal and business assets, creditors approached the court and claimed Ramesh's personal property.

In Suresh's case (Private Limited Company):

His Company faced the loss, but his personal assets remained untouched. The Company's liability was limited to the extent of the business's capital investment. Suresh's personal house and savings were safe. The loss was confined to the Company, and Suresh could restructure and continue his business journey.

Conclusion:

This story clearly illustrates why limited liability is a crucial benefit for business owners. While both friends faced the same business risk, the choice of structure determined the impact on their personal lives.

****

Similar is the case with **Partnership firms.** The only difference is that in the case of proprietorship, the burden lies on a single owner, but in the case of a Partnership Firm, personal liability is shared among partners in their Profit-loss sharing ratios.

Still, many would argue that our business is still not at such a scale as to operate as a company. There are too many compliance and mandatory audits, and so on. But, after understanding this concept of limited liability, they don't want to continue as a proprietorship or partnership firm. So what's the Solution?

The Solution is a **Limited Liability Partnership.**

Just like a partnership firm, it is managed by two or more people who own and manage the affairs of the business. Similar to a company, it enjoys the benefit of limited liability, but there are no two levels of Management. Partners are the owners and decision-makers of an LLP.

Now let's suppose 4 people want to start an LLP, but only two of them will be managing the affairs of the firm, the third is coming in as an investor, and the fourth partner is a celebrity who is a sleeping partner and is in the firm only for building brand image.

In such a case, all four partners will be owners of the business with limited liability, but the first two partners will identify themselves as Designated Partners.

As designated partners, they will be allotted a Designated Partner Identification Number (DPIN) and will be responsible for managing the day-to-day operations of the business. The other two are not required to obtain the DPIN and will be partners of the LLP.

In the LLP, compliances are comparatively low, and there is a threshold of 40 lakhs turnover or capital of more than 25 lakhs under which audit is not mandatory.

Now, how do you decide what is better for your Business, Company, or LLP?

To answer that question, we need to understand the multiple types of Companies. Broadly, a company can be of two types - Public Limited Company and Private Limited Company.

A **Private Limited Company** is generally a family or close friends-run business. As per the laws, a private limited company should have a minimum of 2 members, but it cannot exceed 200.

Whereas a **Public Limited company** needs a minimum of 7 members, there is no capping of maximum members. Public limited companies can be further divided into 2 types, i.e., Listed and Unlisted Public limited companies.

Listed companies are those in which the public has invested money through Stock Exchanges. Whereas **Unlisted Public Limited**'s shares are not traded on stock exchanges.

Now, having understood this, let's answer our main question - **Company vs LLP**.

This decision majorly depends on whether the business intends to raise funds through investors in the future. An investor would like to invest in the Company and hold proportionate shares as per agreed upon valuation.

Otherwise, businesses are advised to go for the LLP model and enjoy hassle-free benefits. If you are wondering, is this the only benefit of limited liability between the proprietorship/partnership model and the company/ LLP model?

The answer is a Big NO !!

There are many other significant benefits of registering business as a Company or a LLP, which are discussed as follows -

1. Business Continuity

Unlike proprietorships, companies enjoy perpetual succession. This means the existence of a company is not affected by changes in ownership or the death of shareholders or directors. The Company continues to exist as a separate legal entity, ensuring stability, reliability, and long-term operations without disruptions.

2. Legacy

A company structure allows the business to outlive its founders and owners, creating a long-lasting legacy. Ownership can be transferred easily through shares, enabling the next generation or professional Management to carry forward the founder's vision and values while scaling the business over decades.

3. ESOP to attract and retain talents

Companies can offer Employee Stock Ownership Plans (ESOPs) — a powerful tool to incentivize employees by giving them ownership stakes in the business. ESOPs attract top talent, improve employee retention, and align employees' interests with business growth, fostering a culture of ownership and loyalty.

4.   Taxability

Proprietorship income is taxed at individual slab rates, which can be high. In contrast, companies are taxed at corporate rates, and they also benefit from various deductions, exemptions, and incentives. Moreover, profits within companies are taxed only at corporate rates, helping in better wealth accumulation and reinvestment.

5.   Funding

Raising capital is significantly easier for companies. They can attract equity investment from venture capitalists, angel investors, and private equity firms. Additionally, banks and financial institutions prefer lending to companies due to their structured governance, audited financial statements, and regulated transparency.

Above, we have discussed a few of the many benefits that will practically impact the majority of businesses.

CHAPTER 6

EARN TAX-FREE INCOME

Have you ever felt that you are paying lots of taxes but still not getting your basic business requirements of funding fulfilled in time of need?

What if I tell you that the Government is offering a scheme where they will fund your businesses without repayment obligation and also take no tax for 3 Years !!!

This Chapter will help you save lakhs of rupees, and I will tell you how to do it.

There is a Startup India recognition scheme; under this scheme, the entity needs to register with the Department for Promotion of Industry and Internal Trade (DPIIT).

This recognition will open the doors for Business of Startup India benefits like -

1. Tax Exemption

A recognized startup, along with registration under Section 80IAC of the Income Tax Act 1961, will get 3-year Tax holidays. This means that out of the first 10 years of incorporation, a startup can choose to avail of tax exemption benefits for any 3 consecutive years.

The limitation to this benefit is that it's available only within the first 10 years of incorporation, and the turnover of the business should not exceed Rs. 100 Crores. And, though a registered partnership firm along with Company and LLP is also eligible to be recognized as a startup, this particular benefit is only available for Startup Registered as a Company or LLP.

2. Self Certification

With the motive to reduce regulatory liabilities over the startups, the Government has provided relief under 6 labor laws and 3 environmental laws. This relief allows self-certification under the laws below and also assures that no physical inspection by departments will be performed for 5 years.

The laws under which these reliefs are available are:

Labour Laws

    a.   The Building and Other Construction Workers (Regulation of Employment and Conditions of Service) Act, 1996

    b.   The Inter-State Migrant Workmen (Regulation of Employment and Conditions of Service) Act, 1979

    c.   The Payment of Gratuity Act, 1972

    d.   The Contract Labour (Regulation and Abolition) Act, 1970

e. The Employees' Provident Funds and Miscellaneous Provisions Act, 1952

f. The Employees' State Insurance Act, 1948

Environmental Laws

a. The Water (Prevention and Control of Pollution) Act, 1974

b. The Water (Prevention and Control of Pollution) Cess Amendment Act, 2003

c. The Air (Prevention & Control of Pollution) Act, 1981

3. Govt Tenders

Startups get access to Government E-Marketplace and are eligible to apply for Government tenders. Under the GeM portal, startups also get a waiver of the requirement to have prior experience for filing tenders, and in many cases, a waiver from payment of earnest money deposit (EMD) is also available.

4. Networking Options

Startups, once recognized with DPIIT, get access to startup groups and associations where they can collaborate with other startups. Collaboratively, they solve common issues and support fellow startups in growing.

New startups also get a headstart through guidance from other startups who have been through those phases.

5.   Research and Innovation benefits

Governments boost growth and research through startups, and for that, they are provided access to incubation centers where they get resources, mentorship, funding opportunities, networking, and a supportive environment, ultimately increasing their chances of success and fostering economic growth.

6.   Patent Application and IPR Protection

To protect the rights of startups in newly developed technology and to help them tap the market fast, up to 80% waiver in fees is provided for filing Patent applications, and their examination processes are also moved through faster channels.

7.   Easy Access to Funds

Startups get much easier access to funds compared to any other business because they drive the economy toward growth through innovation. Startups may get the funds through either of the following methods -

a.   The Government of India has set aside funds of 10,000 crore to seed fund eligible startups.

b.   Investors are generally interested in investing in startup companies for two reasons - first, they become part of a unicorn company during the early phase. Secondly, tax benefits are available for investing in equity share capital of startups.

c. The government also provides credit guarantees to eligible startups so that they can avail themselves of loans up to 20 crores without collateral under credit guarantee schemes of the government.

d. Many big private players and the government announce various challenges frequently under which startups can participate and get market validation of their ideas, and winners of those challenges also win grants.

8. Faster Exit

At times, when business ideas don't succeed, getting an exit from any other business registered as a company is a tiresome task with lots of processes, but for the Company recognized as a startups under DPIIT, this process is smoothened and winding up is completed within 90 days.

There are many other benefits that a startup can gain by being part of the community and having access to investors and other successful companies.

Aren't these benefits interesting?

After reading about all this, many readers would want to get their business registered under DPIIT and would want to avail of the benefits listed above. There are a few eligibility criteria that are mandatory for applying for Startup India recognition.

1. Entity should be registered as a Company, LLP, or a Registered Partnership firm. Tax exemption is not available for registered partnership firms.

2. Startup recognition is only provided within 10 years of incorporation of an entity.

3. Business has to be working in these four areas to be eligible,

   a. Innovation, development, or improvement of new or existing products.

   b. Employment generation

   c. Wealth creation

   d. Solving problems of society

Having understood the concept of a startup, readers should start analyzing your business and how these benefits can be availed.

CHAPTER 7

BUILD STRONG BRAND

These days, businesses start with very catchy and attractive brand names. They spend years making their mark in the market. But when they grow and people start trusting the name, one of two things happens -

1. Either a competition comes up with the same or similar name and replicates the business model. The time, money, and energy invested by the business is exploited by the competitor, and they enjoy good market returns.

2. Or, if the brand on which the business has built its image is not wisely chosen and it also distinctively matches any big MNC, then the business owner may face a case, litigation, or raid by a big player.

****

These scenarios can be easily understood with an example -

Rajat, an ambitious entrepreneur from Nagpur, launched a health food brand called "Nova Nutri." He worked tirelessly for over two years — perfecting recipes, investing in premium packaging, building a strong online presence, and gaining loyal customers.

His brand started appearing on shelves in multiple cities, and "Nova Nutri" became a local success story.

Part 1: The Replication Trap

A few months into his growth phase, a new brand appeared in the same market — "Nova Nature." It offered similar products, with packaging and branding that closely resembled his.

Customers began confusing the two brands. Some distributors accidentally placed the wrong products. The reputation Rajat had worked so hard to build was now indirectly benefitting someone else — a competitor who had observed and replicated his entire business model.

Part 2: The Legal Shock

Just as Rajat was dealing with market confusion, a bigger problem emerged.

A legal notice arrived from a well-known multinational company claiming ownership over the word "Nova" in the health and nutrition space. They accused Rajat of unauthorized usage, demanded he immediately stop selling under the name "Nova Nutri," and threatened litigation for damages.

Rajat was stunned. He had no intention of copying anyone. However, since the MNC had a prior registered right over the name, his intention didn't matter.

The Consequence

Rajat faced the worst of both worlds:

- His brand identity was being exploited by a lookalike competitor, and

- He was facing potential litigation from a powerful corporation.

The years he had spent building a business were now hanging by a thread — not because of market failure, but because he never secured legal ownership of his brand.

****

The Solution

The simple solution to the problems discussed above is to get your brand registered. Trademark registration provides strong protection to your brand & it helps a Growing Business. A Small (™) or ® on the top right corner of your brand name or logo makes all the difference in the following ways -

1. Legal Protection and Exclusive Rights:

A registered trademark grants you exclusive rights to use the mark for the registered goods or services, preventing others from using the same or similar mark without your permission. This legal protection allows you to take action against infringement, ensuring that your brand identity remains unique and protected.

2. Brand Recognition and Differentiation:

Trademark registration enhances brand visibility and recognition, helping consumers identify your products or services and differentiate them from competitors. This can lead to increased consumer trust and loyalty, as a registered trademark signifies a level of quality and reliability.

3. Asset Creation and Value:

A registered trademark becomes a valuable asset for your business, representing intellectual property and goodwill. This asset can be used for licensing, franchising, or even as collateral for loans.

4. Cost-Effectiveness and Long-Term Protection:

Trademark registration in India is relatively inexpensive, offering long-term protection for your brand. The trademark is valid for 10 years from the date of registration and can be renewed indefinitely for successive 10-year periods.

5. Other Benefits:

Trademark registration helps in marketing and promotion, as it establishes a strong brand identity that is easily recognizable. It can also attract customers and build a positive reputation for your business.

Trademarks are investments that will shield the brand for years and provide competitive protection to the business.

CHAPTER 8

REGISTRATIONS TO GROW SALES

Businesses face difficulty in growing their sales significantly. Survival of businesses is mostly dependent on local buyers. What they miss is the opportunities available outside local markets.

In the Chapter, we have discussed two such impactful registrations that will help businesses grow their sales.

GeM Registration

There was a big entry block in becoming a Government supplier. Many eligible businesses also didn't get tenders.

But this recent move by the Government has opened doors to Tender bidding for all. The government has introduced an online portal called Government E-Market (GeM). This portal provides single-window access to businesses to showcase their products and services and participate in tenders.

This is a must-have registration, and the process to obtain registration is as simple as making an email ID. This registration will help in tapping great opportunities.

Global Market (Import Export Code)

Similar to the requirement of GeM registration to supply to the Government, there is a registration that will give business owners access to Global Markets.

It's the Import Export Code; just like a person needs a license to drive a vehicle, A business needs IEC to export goods/ services globally. There are lots of Government schemes for the promotion of exports.

The major benefits of working through the GeM portal and in the Global Market are -

1. **Expansion of Market Reach**

    a. GeM enables access to a wide base of government buyers (central, state, PSUs).

    b. IEC unlocks global markets, allowing businesses to export goods and services worldwide.

    c. Together, they diversify sales channels and reduce dependence on local markets.

2. **Raising Quality Standards**

    a. Supplying to government or international buyers involves stringent quality checks, certifications, and compliance.

    b. This naturally pushes businesses to upgrade their products and processes.

c.   These improvements also create opportunities to launch a premium product line in the domestic market.

3. Enhanced Business Credibility

a.   Both registrations act as trust symbols — showing that the business is compliant, registered, and qualified for regulated markets.

b.   Improves brand image among private, institutional, and B2B clients.

4. Standardization and Process Improvement

a.   Adhering to GeM or export guidelines requires businesses to adopt proper SOPs, inventory controls, labeling, packaging, and documentation systems.

b.   This leads to greater operational efficiency and preparedness for audits or scaling.

5. Better Pricing and Volume Opportunities

a.   Government and foreign orders are usually placed in bulk and often at competitive or premium prices.

b.   This enables better margins and economies of scale, especially for manufacturers and wholesalers.

6. **Eligibility for Incentives and Financial Schemes**

   a. IEC holders can avail of export-related incentives under schemes like RoDTEP, Advance Authorisation, SEIS, etc.

   b. GeM sellers may get benefits like vendor ratings, loan schemes, and preference in procurement under the Make in India initiative.

7. **Competitive Edge in the Local Market**

   a. Export or government supply experience becomes a differentiator in local markets — helping the business build a reputation as a quality player.

   b. It also enables better domestic pricing strategies due to higher perceived value.

8. **Access to High-Value Tenders and Institutional Orders**

   a. GeM registration is mandatory for participating in many government tenders, including infrastructure, education, medical, and IT supply.

   b. IEC opens up B2B collaboration with international buyers, e-commerce platforms, and import-export houses.

9. **Stronger Compliance and Documentation Framework**

   a. Both registrations bring discipline in terms of legal compliance, invoice format, logistics documentation, and regulatory reporting, reducing future risks.

10. **Business Scalability and Investment Readiness**

   a. With both registrations, the business becomes more structured, transparent, and growth-ready.

   b. This attracts investors, banks, and joint venture partners due to improved governance and market exposure.

CHAPTER 9

MISCELLANEOUS BUT IMPORTANT

Here, we will discuss a few miscellaneous licenses and registrations which are applicable to all types of businesses. Non-compliance with these could lead to penalties and actions against businesses.

1. Trade Licences

A trade license is an official document issued by a local municipal corporation or governing body granting permission to individuals or entities to conduct business activities within a specific geographic area.

It's a form of authorization that ensures businesses operate legally and comply with local regulations. Obtaining a trade license helps ensure that businesses adhere to local laws, regulations, and safety standards.

Trade licenses help prevent the exploitation of employees, reduce the risk of fire-related accidents, ensure fair trade practices, safeguard consumers, and support business growth by establishing credibility.

Trade licenses are typically valid for one year and require renewal. Operating with an expired license can lead to fines or legal action.

2.   Shop and Establishment Licence

The Shop and Establishment Act regulates the shops and commercial establishments operating within the state. Every state has its own Shop and Establishment Act ("Act"). However, the general provisions of the Act are the same in all states. The Labour Department of the respective states implements the Shop and Establishment Act.

The proprietors who run a business from home without having any physical store or premises are also required to obtain this Certificate. The proprietors of e-commerce businesses, online businesses, or online stores and establishments must register under this Act and obtain the Certificate. Every shop and commercial establishment should register itself under the Act within 30 days of the commencement of business.

The Certificate or the Shop License acts as a basic registration/license for the business. This Certificate is produced to obtain many other business licenses and registrations. It serves as proof of the incorporation of commercial establishments or shops. It is also useful when the proprietor of the business wants to obtain a loan or create a current bank account for the business. Most banks will ask for this Certificate to open a current bank account.

The Act, among other things, regulates the following matters-

- Hours of work, annual leave, weekly holidays.

- Payment of wages and compensation.

- Prohibition of employment of children.

- Prohibition of employing women and young persons on the night shift.

- Enforcement and Inspection.

- Interval for rest.

- Opening and closing hours.

- Record keeping by the employers.

- Dismissal provisions.

You may now wonder why the Trade Licence and Shop Establishment Licence seem similar. But both are very different, and here is the comparison between **Trade License** and **Shop & Establishment License**:

Point of Difference	Trade License	Shop and Establishment License
Governing Authority	Issued by the Municipal Corporation	Issued by the Labour Department or Local Government
Purpose	To regulate specific trades and ensure public safety and compliance	To regulate working conditions of employees in shops and commercial establishments

Who It Applies To	Businesses engaged in specific trades such as food, manufacturing, and cyber cafés.	All shops, commercial establishments, and even home-based businesses
Type of Properties Covered	Only commercial properties	Both commercial and residential properties
Registration Timeframe	Must be obtained before starting the trade	Must be obtained within 30 days of commencing operations
Key Features	- Ensures ethical business practices - Enforces safety laws	- Regulates work hours, leave policies, wages, and working conditions
Industry Examples	Hotels, restaurants, manufacturing units, food stalls, cyber cafés	Retail shops, service providers, online businesses, small offices
Employee Welfare Regulations	Does not cover employee working conditions	Covers employee rights, including working hours, rest periods, holidays, and child labor rules
Requirement Under	Legal requirements for conducting specific types of business	Mandatory registration for every place of business not covered under the Factories Act, 1948

State-Specific Regulations	Varies by state	Varies by state

3. <u>Labor Law Registrations</u>

Labor is one of the most valuable assets in any organization. To ensure a healthy, fair, and secure working environment, the Indian Government has enacted a comprehensive framework of labor laws aimed at regulating employer-employee relationships. These laws are crucial not only for protecting the rights and welfare of workers but also for ensuring that businesses operate within a compliant and ethical framework.

Labor laws in India are governed by both the Central and State Governments and apply to different types of establishments depending on factors such as the number of employees, nature of work, and industry. There are over 30 central labor legislations and numerous state-specific rules covering areas such as wages, working hours, industrial relations, maternity benefits, employee safety, contract labor, and social security.

While many labor laws are sector-specific, certain laws are universally applicable to all establishments that meet basic thresholds. Among these, three key registrations stand out as essential for any business employing workers:

****

1. Employees' State Insurance (ESI) Registration

Applicability:

- Mandatory for establishments employing 10 or more employees (in some states, the threshold is 20), earning wages up to ₹21,000 per month.

- Governed under the Employees' State Insurance Act 1948.

Benefits to Employees:

- **Medical Benefits**: Full medical care to the insured and their dependents.

- **Sickness Benefits**: Cash compensation during certified sickness.

- **Maternity Benefits**: Paid leave and medical care for insured women.

- **Disability Benefits**: Monthly pensions for temporary or permanent disablement due to employment injury.

- **Dependents' Benefit**: Pensions to dependents in case of death due to employment injury.

Consequences of Non-Compliance:

- The penalty of up to ₹5,000 per default.

- Interest on delayed contributions and potential imprisonment under serious violations.

- Prosecution for failure to pay dues or maintain required records.

****

2. Employees' Provident Fund (EPF) Registration

Applicability:

- Mandatory for establishments employing 20 or more employees.

- Covered under the Employees' Provident Funds and Miscellaneous Provisions Act, 1952.

- Optional for establishments with fewer employees, but once registered, compliance is mandatory.

Benefits to Employees:

- **Retirement Corpus**: A portion of salary is accumulated with employer contribution for retirement.

- **Pension Scheme (EPS)**: Monthly pension for eligible employees post-retirement.

- **Insurance (EDLI)**: Life insurance covers nominees in case of the employee's death.

- **Partial Withdrawals**: Allowed for specific needs like housing, marriage, or education.

Consequences of Non-Compliance:

- **Interest and damages** on late payment of contributions (up to 25% damages).

- **Prosecution** and **penal action** under the Act, which may include **imprisonment of up to 3 years**.

- **Inspection and audit** by EPFO officials leading to reputational harm.

****

3. Payment of Gratuity Registration

Applicability:

- Applicable to every establishment employing 10 or more employees.

- Governed by the Payment of Gratuity Act, 1972.

Benefits to Employees:

- A lump-sum payment to employees as a token of appreciation for long-term service (minimum 5 years).

- Payable at the time of retirement, resignation, death, or disablement.

- The gratuity amount is calculated as:

- (15 / 26) × Last drawn salary × Years of service

Consequences of Non-Compliance:

- Employers may be directed to pay with interest from the due date.

- Penalty up to ₹10,000 or imprisonment up to 1 year for avoiding payment.

- Legal action may be initiated by the employee or Labour Commissioner.

****

Why Labour Law Compliances Matter

- **Legal Requirement**: Non-compliance attracts penalties, prosecution, and closure risks.

- **Trust and Retention**: Ensuring employee welfare builds goodwill, morale, and loyalty.

- **Operational Continuity**: Prevents disruption due to legal proceedings or strikes.

- **Contract Eligibility**: Many government and corporate contracts require strict labor compliance.

****

Summary of Other Important Labor Laws (Brief Mention)

Although our primary focus is on ESIC, EPF, and Gratuity, it is important to be aware of several other crucial laws in the labor framework:

Category	Key Laws
Wages and Bonus	Minimum Wages Act, 1948; Payment of Wages Act, 1936; Payment of Bonus Act, 1965
Employment Terms	Industrial Disputes Act, 1947; Contract Labour Act, 1970
Safety & Welfare	Factories Act, 1948; BOCW Act, 1996
Women & Children	Maternity Benefit Act, 1961; Child Labour Act, 1986
Social Security	Employees' Compensation Act, 1923; Unorganized Workers' Social Security Act, 2008

Towards Simplification: New Labor Codes

In 2020, the Government of India passed four labor codes to consolidate 29 existing laws, aiming to simplify registration and compliance processes:

1.   Code on Wages, 2019

2.   Code on Social Security, 2020

3.   Code on Occupational Safety, Health and Working
     Conditions, 2020

4.   Industrial Relations Code, 2020

While these codes are yet to be implemented uniformly across all states,
they signal a shift toward the "One registration, One return"
framework—significantly easing the compliance burden for employers.

Conclusion

Thank You for reading it till the end; before we conclude - Let's summarise the key takeaways from the book, which will work as a quick guide for the readers.

Registration 1

We started with the basic but important concept of **PAN**, in which key points were understood about the mandatory requirements of applying for and quoting PAN. We also discussed the penalty of non-compliance and discussed a case study.

Registration 2

Next, the topic covered the concept of **MSME** and how this is helping small businesses maintain strong liquidity. Also, classification criteria are discussed, which will help readers in analyzing their position in this scheme.

Registration 3

A secret tool of **HUF** that can be used to save tax, we saw with a case study how more than 40% of tax was saved through this strategy. The strategy to use this tool in succession planning was also covered.

Registration 4

A well-known concept of **GST** was discussed, and we understood a different perspective on how it can be used for benefit. Also, mandatory registration requirements under the Act were discussed.

Registration 5

This is the most impactful discussion as it works on the wrong beliefs of the majority of business owners in India. Detailed discussion on the concept of a **Body Corporate,** along with its benefits over proprietorship and partnership, were discussed.

Registration 6

All about **Startup recognition,** along with its various benefits, were understood in this topic.

Registration 7

Here, we have the solution to the terrifying mistake of losing a brand built by decades of hard work. Various benefits of **trademark** registration are noted.

Registration 8

GeM Registration opens doors for businesses to supply to the Government and its various benefits.

Registration 9

Import Export Code and related registration help businesses go global and raise quality parameters, along with many benefits.

Registration 10

Trade Licence's mandatory requirements along with its scope and compliances.

Registration 11

Shop, Establishment license - Requirement, process, scope, benefits, and non-compliance penalties were discussed.

Registration 12

Labor law-related mandatory registration will also help avoid non-compliance and retain employees. Focused discussion of 3 main laws: EPF, ESIC, and Gratuity Act.

****

I thank all the readers for reaching out here; there are two categories of readers, and the value you will gain from this book is directly dependent on the category you fall into.

First, some readers are very comfortable with old business methods and are reluctant to adapt to change. They don't want to upgrade their beliefs and end up staying behind the competition. In recent years, many new startups have just started and surpassed decade-old business houses that are not implementing the knowledge they gain.

Then comes the second category of action takers; trust me, if you are in this category, then you are in for exponential growth. They work upon the new knowledge gained and implement it in their business. They save ethically on taxes, interest, and penalties. Save themselves from unlimited liabilities and take advantage of government schemes to build a brand and grow sales.

I urge you all to be action-takers and Wish you unimaginable growth in your business.

CONNECT WITH THE AUTHOR 

I would be honored to help you all with any queries you have regarding the concepts discussed in the book. To get more clarity on any topic that you found insightful, please feel free to reach out to us. I would love to read your positive feedback and learn about the value you gained from this book.

Email id - contact@caashutoshagrawal.com

Continue being updated on tax, commerce, and economics, and get in touch with the author. Scan QR to follow the WhatsApp channel -